# THE PRINCIPLES OF DEMOCRACY

# WHAT IS FAIRNESS?

 JOSHUA TURNER

New York

Published in 2020 by The Rosen Publishing Group, Inc.
29 East 21st Street, New York, NY 10010

Copyright © 2020 by The Rosen Publishing Group, Inc.

All rights reserved. No part of this book may be reproduced in any form without permission in writing from the publisher, except by a reviewer.

First Edition

Editor: Melissa Raé Shofner
Book Design: Reann Nye

Photo Credits: Seriest art Bplanet/Shutterstock.com; cover andresr/E+/Getty Images; p. 5 ESB Professional/Shutterstock.com; p. 7 Kraig Scarbinsky/DigitalVision/Getty Images; p. 9 H. Armstrong Roberts/ClassicStock/Getty Images; p. 11 Susan Montgomery/Shutterstock.com; p. 13 Burlingham/Shutterstock.com; p. 15 Image Source/Photodisc/Getty Images; p. 17 Hill Street Studios/Blend Images/Getty Images; p. 19 Toa55/Shutterstock.com; p. 21 Nic Neufeld/Shutterstock.com; p. 22 Robert Kneschke/Shutterstock.com.

Cataloging-in-Publication Data

Names: Turner, Joshua.
Title: What is fairness? / Joshua Turner.
Description: New York : PowerKids Press, 2020. | Series: The principles of democracy | Includes glossary and index.
Identifiers: ISBN 9781538342725 (pbk.) | ISBN 9781538342749 (library bound) | ISBN 9781538342732 (6 pack)
Subjects: LCSH: Fairness–Juvenile literature. | Democracy–Juvenile literature. | Conduct of life–Juvenile literature.
Classification: LCC BJ1533.F2 T87 2019 | DDC 179'.9-dc23

Manufactured in the United States of America

CPSIA Compliance Information: Batch #CSPK19: For Further Information contact Rosen Publishing, New York, New York at 1-800-237-9932

# CONTENTS

WHAT IS FAIRNESS?............4
DOES FAIR MEAN EQUAL?.........6
WHAT IS UNFAIR?..............8
FAIRNESS IN EVERYDAY LIFE......10
FAIRNESS IN A DEMOCRACY......12
GETTING WHAT YOU WANT........14
LIFE ISN'T ALWAYS FAIR.........16
BEING FAIR TO OTHERS..........18
BEING FAIR TO OURSELVES.......20
WHY FAIRNESS IS IMPORTANT.....22
GLOSSARY....................23
INDEX.......................24
WEBSITES....................24

# WHAT IS FAIRNESS?

In a fair society, everyone is treated in a just way and given a chance to succeed. People treat others the way they want others to treat them. Fairness is especially important in a democracy, which is a type of government in which the people rule and honesty and justice are valued.

For many people, life in the United States hasn't always been fair. Through the power of democracy, however, our country can become a fairer place for everyone to live.

### THE SPIRIT OF DEMOCRACY

The United States has an **unfortunate** history of being unfair. For example, it's often harder for poor people to get into college. Today, there are programs in place to help give them the same educational opportunities as others.

Fairness means everyone lives by the same rules and gets a chance to show what they're able to do.

# DOES FAIR MEAN EQUAL?

When a society is fair, it means each person is treated in the way that best allows him or her to succeed. In order to be fair you need to understand that everyone has different strengths, weaknesses, and needs.

Equality is often confused with fairness, but they're not the same. When there's equality in a society, it means every person is treated exactly the same. Giving everyone equal treatment is good if people are very similar, but it's less helpful when there are large differences.

### THE SPIRIT OF DEMOCRACY

A fair society won't always be equal, and an equal society won't always be fair.

In order for a society to be fair, it can't always be equal. This is why children don't live by the same set of rules as adults.

7

# WHAT IS UNFAIR?

When a **situation** is missing the qualities of fairness, we say that it's unfair. It's important to understand that just because situations are fair for some people, doesn't mean they're fair for all people.

No country is completely fair all the time, and this is true for the United States. Unfair could mean African Americans are not given work because of the color of their skin, or the poor can't get a job because they don't have nice clothing.

### THE SPIRIT OF DEMOCRACY

Being fair is often hard, especially in a large society such as the United States. What one group of people sees as fair may seem unfair to another group. It can be hard to make everyone happy.

Early **unions** worked toward fair treatment for their members in the work place. They continue to fight for workers' rights today.

9

# FAIRNESS IN EVERYDAY LIFE

In a fair society, rules and laws apply equally to all people at all times. It would be unfair if certain parts of society had different laws for the same situations.

Imagine a famous person who gets a speeding ticket being **punished** differently than a regular citizen who commits the same crime. Or two people being paid different amounts of money for doing the same job because one person is a man and the other is a woman. These situations aren't fair, but they happen.

> In a fair society, the rules are the same for everyone. If some people didn't have to stop at a red light, driving would be unfair, not to mention very dangerous.

# FAIRNESS IN A DEMOCRACY

A democracy is a type of government in which every person has a say. The United States is a type of democracy called a republic. In a republic, citizens vote for **representatives** to stand for them in government.

In a fair democracy every person gets one vote and all votes count the same. It wouldn't be fair if votes of wealthy people or people who owned property counted more than those of others.

### THE SPIRIT OF DEMOCRACY

The United States isn't perfect, but it has still tried to set an example of what a fair democracy is to the rest of the world for over 200 years.

Having an equal vote in an election is key to achieving fairness in a democracy.

# GETTING WHAT YOU WANT

A situation in which you don't get what you want can still be fair, even though you might feel otherwise. For example, you may choose to **support** your friend who's running for class president. You may even help out with her **campaign**.

However, after all the votes are counted, your friend may still lose. Everyone's votes counted equally, and everyone had the chance to tell others to vote. This means that even if your friend loses, the election was still fair.

> Even if a situation is fair, you still might not get what you want.

# LIFE ISN'T ALWAYS FAIR

Life in any democratic society won't always be fair. Some people may be **prejudiced**. Other people may try to cheat to get what they want. This means people need to work hard to understand how life isn't fair for others and try to change it.

Understanding other peoples' lives and trying to help has been the key to **activist** movements in our country's history. People who are treated well need to help those who are being treated unfairly fight for change.

### THE SPIRIT OF DEMOCRACY

The United States has slowly become fairer over time. Voting rights were first **extended** from land-owning white males to all white males and eventually to **minorities** and women. Today, any U.S. citizen can vote.

An important part of being a citizen is doing your best to make society fairer for everyone.

# BEING FAIR TO OTHERS

Treating others the way you would like to be treated is the key to fairness. This means putting yourself in the position of others and imagining how you would feel. This is called empathy, and it's an important part of having a fair society.

An elected official must make laws for all of society. In order for the laws to be fair, elected officials need to have empathy for people who are in different situations or have different backgrounds from themselves.

> Treating others the way you would want to be treated in a similar situation is an important part of a fair society. In fact, this basic belief is called the "golden rule."

# BEING FAIR TO OURSELVES

It's important to treat other people fairly, but it's also important to be fair to ourselves. Recognizing that a situation is unfair for you is a key part of making change in a democracy. It allows a person to understand what part of a situation is unfair and how to best tell other people about it.

Fighting for a fairer society will help everyone. It starts with understanding how the unfair situation hurts you and thinking about how it might also be hurting others.

> Workers' rights movements began because workers realized they were being treated unfairly. Any laws passed helped all workers and created a fairer workplace for everyone.

# WHY FAIRNESS IS IMPORTANT

A democracy depends on people making choices about their government and how they want to live, so it's important for everyone to have a fair chance at being heard. An unfair democracy means that some voices aren't heard and some **experiences** aren't understood.

Laws should be fair to all people and all citizens should be given the same opportunities to succeed. A democracy depends on its citizens to be active members of their community in order to know who is being treated fairly and who is not.

# GLOSSARY

**activist:** Someone who acts strongly in support of or against an issue.

**campaign:** A series of activities designed to produce a particular result.

**experience:** Something that you have done or that has happened to you.

**extend:** To make something available to someone.

**minority:** A group of people who are different from the larger group in a country or other area in some way, such as race or religion.

**prejudiced:** Having unfair feelings of dislike for a person or group because of race or religious or political beliefs.

**punish:** To make someone suffer for a crime.

**representative:** Someone who acts or speaks for or in support of another person or group.

**situation:** All the facts, conditions, and events that affect someone or something in a certain time and place.

**support:** To hold up and help.

**unfortunate:** Not appropriate or desirable.

**union:** An organization of workers formed to protect the rights and interests of its members.

# INDEX

**A**
activism, 16

**C**
campaign, 14

**E**
empathy, 18
equality, 6

**L**
laws, 10

**P**
prejudice, 16

**R**
representative, 12
republic, 12

**S**
success, 4, 6

**U**
unfair, 8, 10, 16, 20

**V**
voting, 12, 14

# WEBSITES

Due to the changing nature of Internet links, PowerKids Press has developed an online list of websites related to the subject of this book. This site is updated regularly. Please use this link to access the list: www.powerkidslinks.com/pofd/fair